BY Q. L. PEARCE

TITAN A.E.

THE REAL SCIENCE BEHIND THE SCIENCE FICTION

TITAN A.E. TM & © 2000 Twentieth Century Fox Film Corporation.
All rights reserved. Published in the USA by Price Stern Sloan, a
member of Penguin Putnam Books for Young Readers, New York.
Printed in the USA.

First published in Great Britain by
HarperCollins*Entertainment* in 2000
HarperCollins*Entertainment* is an imprint of
HarperCollins*Publishers* Ltd, 77-85 Fulham Palace Road,
Hammersmith, London W6 8JB

The HarperCollins website address is
www.**fire**and**water**.com

Book Design: Fred Fehlau

ISBN 0 00 710312 3

THE REAL SCIENCE BEHIND THE SCIENCE FICTION

TRY to imagine what life on Earth and in space will be like 1,000 years from now. It's pretty difficult, isn't it? Will humans be vacationing and living on the moon—or on the moons of Saturn or Jupiter? Will creatures from distant galaxies be sharing our home planet?

Welcome to the world of *Titan A.E.* This movie is an adventure story that gives you an idea of some possibilities for the future. *Titan A.E.* takes you on a journey with Cale, the hero, Akima, the pilot, and their comrades through the distant reaches of space in search of the spaceship *Titan*. And what does A.E. stand for, you ask? The answer is, *After Earth*.

The film starts off in the year 3023, just as the evil Drej have destroyed the Earth. Cale's father, Sam Tucker, created the *Titan*, a massive ship that is the only hope for humankind. The *Titan* holds the secrets to survival. Cale is the only person who can find it, and he has to battle the Drej every step of the way.

In order to create this fantastic story, plenty of real science was involved. This book offers a look into the facts that make telling this story possible. For example, is it possible to exist without a planet? Where could we go? What does space have to offer us?

Fortunately for us humans, the movie *Titan A.E.* is fiction. But that doesn't mean that someday—far, far in the future—creepy beings like the Drej won't threaten our planet. So until then, sit back, find a comfy chair, and get ready for an action-packed, science-filled experience like you've never had before. Oh, and by the way—in case you get stumped on a word or concept—there is a really cool and informative glossary in the back of the book. See you in space!

SPACECRAFT

IF the Earth's population were suddenly faced with leaving the home **planet**, where would they go? How would they get there? At the beginning of the third millennium in *Titan A.E.*, the Drej have attacked Earth, and all of its inhabitants have boarded spaceships in a desperate race for survival. Luckily for them, **space** travel started being developed in the twentieth century.

Getting off the surface of the planet isn't easy. Earth's **gravity** keeps everything from flying out into space and makes it very difficult to launch a heavy spacecraft into **orbit**. Gravity is a **force** that attracts every object in the **universe** to every other object. An object has to have a lot of **mass** before the effect of its gravity is easy to notice. Also, the closer objects are to each other, the more the force of gravity will be felt. One way to slip from gravity's grip is to go very, very fast. For a ship to break free and zoom into orbit, it must go nearly 18,000 miles per hour. How can you get a ship moving that fast? Rocket engines are the answer. They send high-pressure **gas** out of one end of the craft, causing the craft to move in the opposite direction.

Space Fact
The first living Earth space traveler was a pint-sized, mixed-breed dog named Laika, Russian for Barker. She rode aboard Sputnik II.

Space Speak
A satellite is an object that circles a larger object in space. The moon is a natural satellite of Earth.

WHAT MAKES IT GO?

Currently spacecraft are lifted from Earth by fuel-burning **rockets** with names such as *Titan* (just like the movie!), *Atlas*, and *Saturn*. The heavier the ship and its cargo, the more muscle the rocket has to have in the form of fuel. A rocket usually carries chemical fuel that needs **oxygen** to make it burn. Oxygen isn't especially easy to come across in space, so spacecraft carry their own. Sometimes they carry liquid oxygen and sometimes they carry a special chemical that combines with oxygen, producing plenty of gas. The gases expand very quickly and shoot out the back of the rocket. This propels the rocket skyward. It's a bit like what happens when you let go of the neck of an inflated balloon. The air escapes from the opening, and the balloon zooms in the opposite direction.

Space Fact
In a ship heading for deep space, the effect of Earth's gravity would lessen as the craft moves farther away.

As the Drej blast Earth, most of humanity evacuates aboard space-bound "buses" that carry dozens of passengers. These escape craft probably function something like the Venture Star,™ a space vehicle that is planned to go into service early in the twenty-first century. Unlike the shuttle, this craft will not drop off fuel tanks and rocket boosters as it soars into orbit, making it completely reusable. By Cale's time, such a vehicle will probably be capable of carrying many passengers in the manner of a twenty-first century passenger plane. It's likely to be inexpensive to use and operate and, therefore, plentiful. That would be a big plus during an evacuation like the one in *Titan A.E.*

In the late
nineteenth century,
William Thomson
(Lord Kelvin) made a
name for himself as
a scientist. It's a
good thing he
wasn't a fortune-
teller because in
1895 he claimed that
heavier-than-air
flight was
impossible.

The ancestors of the huge spacecraft of Cale's time are the space shuttles *Columbia*, *Challenger*, *Discovery*, *Atlantis*, and *Endeavour*. The type of space shuttle presently used is boosted into orbit by two huge rockets and rides on top of a giant outer fuel tank. After the launch, the rockets fall off and parachute back to Earth. The only part that is disposable is the fuel tank. It drops off and breaks up over the ocean.

WHERE DOES SPACE BEGIN?

Earth's **atmosphere** extends for more than 100 miles above the surface of the planet, though it is very thin at the upper levels. To be given the title of astronaut, you have to fly more than fifty miles up. Some scientists think space begins at the point at which a spacecraft starts to heat up during **reentry** into Earth's atmosphere. That takes place at about seventy-five miles above the surface of the Earth. The spacecraft heats up because as the ship passes through the atmosphere, it creates friction, a force that slows the movement of the craft and produces heat. ◎

TITAN

Height: *11,200 ft / 3,414 m*
Diameter: *5,000 ft / 1,524 m*
The most advanced Earth ship ever built, it was the centerpiece of humankind's plan to protect their species against an uncertain future. Its full potential is yet to be discovered.

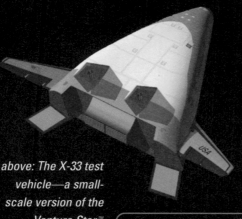

above: The X-33 test vehicle—a small-scale version of the Venture Star.™ The X-33 is half the size and one quarter the cost of the Venture Star.™ right: The X-33, the Venture Star,™ the space shuttle.

It took a very powerful rocket to make the lunar trip possible. The Saturn V was up to the job. As tall as the Great Pyramid of Egypt, it weighed 3,000 tons at liftoff, most of that in fuel. With a great shudder, its five huge engines spouted flame and boosted the craft into the clear blue sky. Most rockets are sent up in connected sections called stages that can be dropped off as their fuel is used up—a practice that will certainly be outdated in Cale's time.

The space shuttle lifts off with reusable solid-fuel booster rockets.

Space Fact
During launch, shuttle astronauts are pressed back in their seats with a force of about 225 pounds. Just before first stage shutdown they feel about four times their normal Earth weight.

CHAPTER 2

FASTER THAN LIGHT

Space Fact
If ships are moving really fast, they must first slow down in order to land. One method of doing this is **aerobraking**. The craft opens a large shield something like an upside-down umbrella that uses the drag of the **atmosphere** to slow the vehicle.

hen the movie *Titan A.E.* opens, we meet young Cale Tucker, a boy separated from his father as Earth's inhabitants flee the evil Drej aliens. Sam Tucker, a scientist and Cale's father, has created a magnificent ship that is the answer to creating a new home **planet**—but he must navigate this ship, the *Titan*, to a safe location where the Drej cannot find it. Meanwhile, Cale and his alien guardian, Tek, make their escape on another **rocket** ship.

In the age of *Titan A.E.*, spacecraft routinely travel from one **star** system to another. Although such travel isn't yet possible, it likely will be developed. Standard fuels can be useful for travel within the solar system, but a manned journey to the stars is going to take something special. The problem is that **space** is really, really huge. The nearest star is incredibly far away. To get anywhere while you're still breathing, you have to travel very fast—faster than the speed of **light** (which is 186,000 miles per second). So far no one has figured out how to do that.

Space Speak
FTL stands for faster than light.

SHORTCUTS IN SPACE

If we can't go faster than light, maybe we could just take a shortcut—such as a **wormhole**. Using a wormhole may be the way that the Drej were able to sneak up so close to Earth with-

Earth's population evacuates in passenger spacecraft able to carry more than one hundred refugees to safety.

out warning. No one knows if wormholes really exist, but in theory, they are deformities in **space-time**—sort of openings between areas of curved space. For example, imagine that you are a tiny gnat that wants to get from one edge of a mile-long sheet of paper to the other edge. (The gnat represents a spaceship and the paper represents space itself.) That could take your puny gnat-sized self a very long time. Now imagine that the paper is bent in half so that the two edges almost meet, and there is a small "wormhole" through both layers of the paper near the double edge. If you simply dropped through the hole, you would travel from one edge of the paper to the opposite edge in the blink of an eye. If wormholes exist, they would be very unstable, but they could serve as such shortcuts. ◎

Space Fact

NASA probe *Deep Space 1*, launched in fall 1998, uses an **ion propulsion** system and carries only about 176 pounds of fuel.

Robert H. Goddard loved rockets. On March 16, 1926, he launched the first liquid fuel rocket from a field in Massachusetts.

Burning liquid oxygen and gasoline, the ten-foot-tall rocket rose about forty feet up and crash landed about 185 feet away from its starting point. In 1935, one of his rockets actually flew faster than the speed of sound. Despite his hard work, Goddard died in 1945, before the first rocket was launched into space.

A DEADLY SPIN

as humans flee their doomed world, the mammoth Drej mothership moves in to deal the final blow. How did the villains of *Titan A.E.* destroy the Earth? As humans abandoned their <u>planet</u>, the Drej dealt it a death blow. By hitting it off center with a tremendous burst of continuous <u>energy</u>, they caused it to spin faster and faster. For a while, <u>gravity</u> and <u>centripetal force</u> hung in balance, then gravity gave way. The planet bulged and lurched, then flew apart. Is such a thing truly possible? Maybe if you have an unlimited supply of energy—and energy is what the Drej are made of.

If the Earth were demolished, the <u>moon</u> would most likely be destroyed as well. It is locked in <u>orbit</u> around our planet and would be seriously bombarded and possibly shattered by rocky debris. If it survived such a beating, its orbit would certainly change, perhaps putting it on a collision course with another <u>space</u> object. In short, scientists have no definite answer concerning what exactly would happen to the

The huge Drej mothership is made up of pure energy, like the Drej themselves. Its main laser cannon releases a killing blast of energy that can destroy planets.

DREJ

Species: *Drej*

History: *Highly intelligent, super-evolved alien species. Having evolved beyond physical form, they are translucent and pulse with fluid energy. They are cold and ruthless killers with no regard for life.*

Mission: *Total domination and control of the universe, and elimination of all rebel factions considered to be a threat to their supremacy.*

Deep inside the earth is a dense, super-heated <u>core</u> that is under incredible pressure. Releasing that pressure at once would be catastrophic.

Space Fact
The Earth does in fact bulge a little at its <u>equator</u>, partly as the result of its <u>rotational speed</u> of about 1,000 miles per hour. Rotational speed is how fast a planet spins on its own axis—an imaginary line drawn through the planet from pole to pole. When Earth was younger, its rotational speed was faster. A day for the early dinosaurs was probably a little more than twenty-three hours long. The effect of the moon's gravity, as well as the drag of the atmosphere and oceans, has helped to slow it down.

moon if the Earth were destroyed. Scientists aren't certain how long the moon has been Earth's companion, but most believe that sometime in the very distant past, Earth smashed into a huge space object at least as big as Mars. It's likely that the moon formed from material ejected from the crash.

Scientists estimate that a scramjet can reach speeds of more than 3,600 miles per hour. Military scramjets could be useful against an off-world enemy like the Drej because they are lightweight and maneuverable.

Some of the Earth defense ships sent to battle the Drej stingers may have been **scramjets**. Now being tested, scramjets only need **hydrogen** fuel. Scramjet is short for **s**upersonic **c**ombustion **ramjet**. They are known as air-breathers because they burn **oxygen** supplied by air scooped from the **atmosphere**. A ramjet has no moving parts. Air enters an opening at the front as it zooms at speeds many times greater than the speed of sound. The air slows once it enters a **combustion area** and is compressed by the forward speed of the aircraft itself. Fuel is injected into the airflow.

WHO ARE THE DREJ?

They are fictitious beings that were created for this movie. The Drej are unique in that they are pure energy. And what's energy? It is the ability to do work. In other words, energy is what makes things happen. Let's look at the <u>sun</u>. It gives off heat and <u>light</u>, which can do work, like make you warm. Heat and sunlight are forms of energy. Energy can't be created or destroyed, only changed from one form to another. Could a life form be energy-based? According to our current concept of life, the answer would be probably no. Still, the frontiers of scientific knowledge are constantly changing, and one of the best scientific tools available is an open mind. ◎

<CHAPTER 4>

TO OUTER SPACE

Titan A.E. brings you in at humanity's darkest hour. Earth has been destroyed, and what is left of the human race is headed for an uncertain future in the depths of **space**. Imagine, like Cale, you sit huddled in a craft amidst terrified **refugees** on a course for—what? What is out there? With the Drej close behind, the humans will have to leave the solar system to find a new home. It's a shame because one of Jupiter's **moons**, Europa, may have signs of life in a watery, ice-capped ocean. And Saturn's largest moon, Titan (like the movie!), could possibly even support an Earth colony for a short time.

Cale and the survivors of the Drej attack must find a new home somewhere else in the **universe**. The universe includes everything we know about and a lot of stuff we've never heard of. As they flee, the survivors pass through their own solar system. Think of it as a galactic neighborhood made up of nine known

Any activity performed by an astronaut or cosmonaut outside of the spacecraft while in orbit is called a spacewalk.

CALE

Species: *Human*
History: *Son of the brilliant scientist Sam Tucker, Cale is a natural inventor. Escaped Earth's destruction at age five. Lost both parents and was raised by an alien named Tek, a friend of his father. Now a rebellious teenager and dock worker on Tau-14.*
Mission: *To use the map genetically encoded on his hand to assist Korso in completing the* Titan *project.*

The Sombrero Galaxy is found in the southern part of the constellation Virgo. It is also known as object M104.

planets and their moons, **asteroids**, **comets**, and a lot of rocks, ice, and dust. The center of attention is the **sun**, a fiery ball of **gas** that contains about ninety-nine percent of the **mass** in the solar system.

When Cale grows up, he will find himself working on a rocky space body called an **asteroid**. An asteroid is a natural object that, in this solar system, circles the sun. Most of the asteroids are in a **ring**, known as the **asteroid belt**, some 150 million miles wide between Mars and Jupiter. They're usually small, but the largest, Ceres, is about 600 miles in diameter. Some space rocks roam outside the regular belt. In August 1989, a very small asteroid zoomed across Earth's path within 400,000 miles of the approaching planet.

TAU-14

In Cale Tucker's time, it is likely that mining colonies would have been set up on large asteroids because they could be a good source of **metal ores**. The asteroid that Cale will call home, Tau-14, is also a convenient site for a repair depot and salvage yard.

DISTANCES IN SPACE

As the getaway ships in *Titan A.E.* enter the great expanses beyond the solar system, feet, yards, and miles have little meaning. Distances in space are so great that a whole new system of measurement is needed. An **astronomical unit**, or AU, is the average distance between the sun and Earth, or about 93 million miles. It would take a person driving a car fifty-five miles per hour about 190 years to travel one AU.

As far as anyone knows, **light** is the fastest thing in the universe. It travels through space at about 186,000 miles per second. A **light-year** is the distance light travels in one Earth year, or about 5,880,000,000,000 miles. That driver mentioned earlier would cover one light-year in about 12.2 million Earth years. If he had plenty of spare time, he might consider driving for 40 million years; then he could cover one parsec, which is equal to about 3.25 light-years. Unfortunately, he would still find himself in empty space because the nearest star, Proxima Centauri, is 4.3 light-years from Earth.

Titan is Saturn's largest moon and the second largest moon in the solar system. It is wrapped in a dense, orange-tinted atmosphere of mainly nitrogen.

Once the *Titan A.E.* spacecraft leaves the solar system and heads for salvation in deep space, how do they know where they are going? A compass certainly won't do them any good. They probably use a "star tracker" system to get an idea of their position. Earth space probe *Deep Space 1* started its journey through the solar system using just such a system to determine what direction it was facing. Although the system has since shut down, the spacecraft had a sensor that could see the sun to help it get a sense of direction. The star tracker recognized patterns of stars, and so helped the craft to figure out the direction it was facing. As the *Titan* zooms to its hiding place, the Earth refugees use the stars to chart a course as far away from the Drej as possible. ◎

As a comet moves close to the sun, it develops a halo of glowing gas and two "tails" that stream out from behind it, one made up of dust and the other of gas.

IT has been fifteen years since Cale raced away from his dying planet. Since then, humans have become nomads, drifting from place to place. With his guardian, Tek, Cale ended up on Tau-14, where he uses his skill with machines to repair or junk damaged vessels. He may not think much about his environment when he is working, but in order to survive in airless space, he needs protection from harmful **radiation**, temperature control, and an **atmosphere** to breathe and regulate air pressure. Such things are provided by his spacesuit. A walk in space is no sweat for Cale. He can work and play in comfort because his spacesuit does everything but make him hot cocoa. On second thought, by the third millennium, there probably will be a hot drink dispenser built into the suit!

Cosmonaut Alexei Leonov was the first man to "walk" in space on March 18, 1965. The brave pioneer opened the _airlock_ on _Voskhod 2_, stepped out into the unknown, then made it back into the spacecraft safe and sound. Since then, working in space has become commonplace.

KORSO

Species: _Human_
History: _Charismatic captain of the_ Valkyrie. _Formerly an officer of the Earth Human Corps, a worldwide legion of soldiers dedicated to the protection of the species from external forces. Awarded Level 1 security clearance for heroic efforts. Worked closely with friend and confidant Sam Tucker on the top-secret_ Titan _project._

Mission: _To find Cale, who possesses the map to the_ Titan_'s hidden location, and guide Cale in ensuring the_ Titan_'s safe retrieval and completion of the project._

An astronaut at work repairing a satellite during a spacewalk. A spacewalk can last up to seven hours.

MMU

Cale's space scooter is a great way to travel. The closest thing we have yet is the **manned maneuvering unit**, or MMU. It is rocket-powered and allows the wearer to move around freely. In 1984, U.S. astronaut Bruce McCandless was the first to move in space without being connected to his spacecraft by a lifeline, or tether. He traveled 330 feet away from his space shuttle and back again without a hitch. Cale can probably travel twice that distance on his scooter without a problem. All he has to do is jump on and ride. The MMU snaps on to the life support system. It is controlled with small **gas** rockets operated by handgrips on the armrests.

MICROGRAVITY

When the lunch bell sounded, Cale showed us how eager he was to get to the head of the line. He took a shortcut through the **docking** bays where ships dock in the **asteroid** space station. On this occasion his timing was a little off, because a huge ship called the *Valkyrie* was also coming in for a landing, knocking Cale head over heels. He drifted freely in space until he was able to get a good grip on the *Valkyrie* with his **gravity** boots. They have magnetic soles that are attracted to the metal skin of the ship, but in spite of their name, they work by magnetic attraction—not gravity.

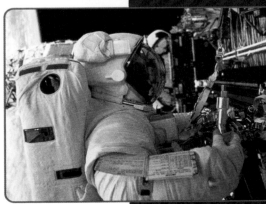

*Cale sometimes complained about his working conditions. He definitely didn't like wasting time in line waiting to get into the station. He wasn't the first to grumble. The first strike in space took place in Skylab in 1974. The crew was unhappy with their work schedule and took a one-day "vacation." **Mission control** quickly came up with a better schedule.*

Matter and Mass

To learn about objects in space, it's important to understand matter. All those neat space objects such as stars, planets, moons, spaceships, and aliens are made up of matter. Matter is everything we can see and/or touch that takes up space and has mass. And what is mass? It's the measure of how much matter something

contains. You can figure out how much mass an object has by weighing it. Imagine a balloon and a bowling ball that are exactly the same size. Which one would you rather have dropped on your foot? The balloon doesn't contain a lot of matter, so it is low mass and very light. The bowling ball is packed with matter, so it has a lot of mass and is very heavy.

To understand what gravity does, you have to know what it doesn't do. Gravity doesn't suck and it doesn't pull—it causes things to fall. When you are on the surface of a planet such as Earth, the **force** of gravity causes your body to fall toward the center of the planet. Fortunately for you, the **solid** crust of the Earth gets in the way and stops your fall. You can measure the effect of gravity as weight. The more **mass** an object has, the greater the effect of gravity and so the heavier it is. When a spacecraft is in **orbit** around the Earth, it has a forward motion, and it is falling toward the planet at the same time. The two motions balance each other out, and the craft stays in orbit. This has a strange side effect on everything inside the ship. Basically, the floor of the craft is falling out from under the feet of the astronauts. They seem to float in the air and are considered weightless, just as Cale was weightless as he momentarily drifted in space near the *Valkyrie*.

Space Fact

There is no such thing as zero gravity. Although it may be so small that it is unnoticeable, the effect of gravity does not disappear completely no matter where in the universe you may go.

Space Fact

Skylab was designed to last nine years, but it fell to Earth in a little over six. It reentered the atmosphere on July 11, 1979, and burned up. Some bits and pieces fell to Earth over the Indian Ocean and Australia—but no one was hurt. In fact, an Australian boy won a $10,000 prize for finding the first official piece.

MIGHTY MUSCLES

While working in space, Cale singlehandedly moved a huge section of a ship that he had been welding. In **microgravity**, not only does Cale experience a feeling of **weightlessness**, but the vessels he works on are also affected by the low gravity. This makes them easier to move with less force.

SPACE STATIONS

Today or one thousand years from now, men and women who live and work in space will need protection and comfort. Space stations such as the one on Tau-14 are the answer. The first space station, *Salyut I*, was launched by the Soviet Union in 1971. It was very simple, with a living area about the size of an average two-car garage. The United States sent *Skylab* spaceside in 1973. Twenty feet long and twenty-one feet wide, *Skylab* was home to three astronauts at a time. It raced in orbit at 17,500 miles per hour, or fast enough to make it from Los Angeles to New York in less than twenty minutes. Two hundred and seventy-five miles above the Earth, astronauts did experiments and made obser-vations in reasonable comfort.

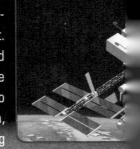

The space stations of the third millennium probably will be much larger and will be able to support a greater population, as well as provide docking ports for many vehicles.

Space Fact
The *Apollo* suits worn on the moon weighed about 180 pounds on Earth. In the moon's light gravity, they were a comfortable thirty pounds.

DOCKING PROCEDURES

When Cale managed to get a look into the *Valkyrie*, he couldn't believe his eyes. The human pilot was the prettiest woman he'd ever seen. She seemed less impressed. After glancing up at him, she closed the blast shields and continued the **docking** procedure. And what's docking? It's the temporary joining of two separate spacecraft. If the *Valkyrie* had not been able to dock, Korso would have had no way to get to Cale and their adventure

might not have begun. To link successfully, the approaching craft must match the other's speed, then line up its docking module with a docking port on the other craft. Slowly, the approaching pilot eases toward the port until the units snap into place, forming an airtight seal. It takes an excellent pilot to dock a craft smoothly—and *Titan A.E.'s* Akima is among the best. ◎

Space Fact
To dock successfully, the docking module on one craft must match the docking port on the other. It's likely that the *Valkyrie* has a universal docking mechanism that can be used at any space station or settlement.

Cale may have had his mind on Akima, but as usual, he was having lunch with Tek. The noisy Tau-14 mess hall was filled with alien beings of many shapes and sizes going about their business. In fact, the cook had a strange resemblance to an over-sized cockroach. Is alien life just the stuff of science fiction? Many scientists don't think so. Some are certain that at least simple forms of life exist beyond our planet. Others believe in the possibility of intelligent life even more advanced than our own.

It's possible that life forms exist that are completely unlike Earth creatures— maybe even some like Tek and the other beings who shared the mess hall with Cale. Still, it's easiest to search for something familiar, so scientists are currently looking for planets with the right conditions for life as we know it on Earth. Planets or moons that have liquid water and an **atmosphere** are at the top of the list. These conditions don't exist on most of the planets and **satellites** in our solar system, but that's no reason to give up hope.

Before His Time
Democritus lived in Greece between 460 B.C. and 370 B.C. He was one of the first people to suggest there were many populated earths in the universe.

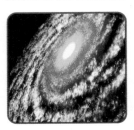

AKIMA
Species: *Human*
History: *No-nonsense pilot of the Valkyrie. Earth refugee. Grew up on a drifter colony where she learned to fly various spacecraft. Her superior flying skills and commanding attitude won her a job piloting the Valkyrie.*
Mission: *To realize the human dream: to find a new home world for humankind.*

Most are sighted between 9:00 and 10:30 in the evening.

Recently some new types of creatures were discovered here on Earth. For the longest time, they were hidden right under the scientists' noses, or rather, right under their feet. In the late 1990s, researchers used a special tool to get a plug of dirt and rock from several hundred feet deep within the Earth's crust. This sample contained living single-**celled** creatures, or bacteria, that were surviving without sunlight or any contact with the surface, and they had probably been down there for millions of years. If Earth life can bury itself away like that, could there be similar bacteria deep within other planets?

MISTAKEN IDENTITY

In 1968, British astronomer Anthony Hewish was among the team of scientists that discovered the first **pulsar**—a spinning **neutron star**. A neutron star is a small, collapsed star made up mostly of very closely packed neutrons. Neutrons are tiny particles found in the center, or nucleus, of an **atom**. Hewish originally thought the regular bursts of **energy** from the pulsar were messages from an intelligent space civilization.

Is there really a chance that there is life beyond our solar system? Will there truly be a time when humans and "off world" life forms live and work together? Is it possible that a society like the Drej has developed on a distant planet? Scientists have studied hundreds of nearby young stars and report that dust rings, which could form into planetary systems, surround many of them. In 1995, a group of Swiss astronomers announced that they had detected the first planet in orbit around a distant star. Since then at least twenty others have been discovered. In 1999, astronomers located a solar system a little like ours some forty-four **light-years** away. It is made up of at least three Jupiter-sized planets and

In 1974, scientists tried to contact life on other planets. They beamed a message from Arecibo, Puerto Rico, toward a cluster of 300,000 stars 25,000 light-years away. The message left the solar system about eight hours after it was sent, but it will travel across space for 25,000 years before it reaches its destination.

Even though Cale lives in space, it's likely that his guardian, Tek, made sure that he got his five servings per day of fresh fruit and vegetables. How was Tek able to do that? With **hydroponics**, the science of growing plants without soil. The plants are raised in water or light gravel with nutrients added. There are a lot of benefits to this kind of agriculture that make it ideal for growing fresh crops on a spacecraft. For example, several different varieties can be grown very close together under artificial light.

The first attempt to listen for signs of intelligent life was made by Frank Drake in 1960. He used an 85-foot radio telescope at the Radio Astronomy Observatory at Green Bank, West Virginia. The **antenna** was aimed at a nearby star, Tau Ceti.

Hydroponic solutions can be used over and over. They must be tested, however, so that water and chemicals can be added as needed.

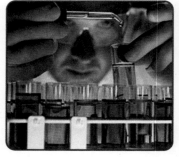

DINING OUT

Cale wasn't crazy about his "fast food" lunch. He thought he was having plain old spaghetti and meatballs, until the "meatballs" started squirming around on his plate and decided to make a break for it. While it's annoying to have your meal jump off your plate, space food has always had drawbacks. Meals the first astronauts ate were in some cases unrecognizable. They included room-temperature, bite-sized cubes, freeze-dried powders, and soft foods squeezed from tubes—not exactly appetizing. Modern astronauts enjoy much better chow, from hot dogs to macaroni and cheese.

PASS THE SALT, PLEASE

Cale showed us in *Titan A.E.* that he has a thing for ketchup (and the cook was definitely unhappy about it!), but certain foods taste better with a little salt and pepper. In **microgravity**, you can't shake spices onto your meal. They won't fall out of the shaker! Instead, pepper comes in liquid form suspended in oil, and salt water is squirted directly into the food.

Water behaves strangely in microgravity. When poured into a glass, it oozes up over the edge. Droplets of water float in the air like silvery bubbles.

The space shuttle kitchen may not have as much room as the one on Tau-14, but it is a real food preparation area with an oven. Menus are healthy and tasty, and the astronauts can even munch on fresh bread, fruit, and ice cream. The food is wrapped in single-serving containers to make it easy to eat in microgravity. Drinks squirt into the mouth from closed containers, and magnetized trays hold knives and forks in place. An astronaut can even strap the tray down. At least the problem of floating (or jumping—ick!) food has been solved. ◎

C ale was interested in meeting the *Valkyrie*'s pretty pilot, but it was the ship's captain who showed up first at just the right time. Korso arrived in the middle of a fight and rescued Cale from two very nasty-tempered aliens. But Korso wasn't just being a nice guy. He knew that Cale held the secret to finding the *Titan*. Cale wasn't immediately interested, but soon found himself in a tight spot looking right down the barrels of Drej **laser** weapons loaded with— **light**! Light may not sound dangerous, but the two space adventurers had to run for their lives.

A laser is used to produce a concentrated beam of light—not like the kind that comes out of a flashlight, but a very narrow beam. Light travels in waves with high and low points like waves in the ocean. The light we see, visible light, is made up of different colors of light. Each color has its own **wavelength**. Usually rays of light spread out and go in different directions as they leave their source, but not laser light. A beam of laser light can be focused in a nearly straight path because, in a laser, the waves of light are all the same color. They go in the same direction and line up exactly, with the high and low points of each wave perfectly matched. The material that produces the light is called the active medium. The first lasers had hearts of **solid** ruby as the active medium.

Space Fact
LASER stands for Light Amplification by Stimulated Emission of Radiation.

PREED

Species: *Akrennian*

History: *Korso's sly alien first mate. Lost his left ear and part of his skull in a wild shootout with slave traders on P'lochda 5 years ago. Met Korso in a back-alley hospital, where Korso was also recovering from laser wounds. The two joined forces, each hoping he had found a trustworthy comrade in a* **galaxy** *without much loyalty.*

Mission: *To assist Korso in all his dealings.*

Lasers can be used in many ways. Carbon dioxide gas lasers slice through metal and fabric alike. Without a blade to wear down, these cutting tools last for a long time. The heat produced by the powerful light beam can be used for welding or attaching two metal pieces together. When Cale worked on spacecraft at Tau-14, he probably used a laser welder.

In the military, lasers are used for communications, laser-guided missiles, and as range finders to determine the distance to a target. Small hand-held laser weapons are called particle-beam weapons. Although they may be very handy for the Drej, for humans they aren't practical yet. Large-scale laser weapons don't work too well, either. When the light hits it, the air around the target warms up, spreads the beam, and makes it less effective.

Science Speak
Wavelength is the distance from one point in a wave to the next similar point. For example—from a low point to the next low point.

Because they travel in a straight, narrow line, laser beams are also handy for measuring distance. If you want to know exactly how far it is to the moon, a laser beam bounced off the lunar surface will give you the answer.

IN MOTION

During his dramatic exit from the commissary on Tau-14, Korso had to think quickly. He and Cale had to get out of the line of Drej fire, but how? They were trapped with no way out, except by obeying the law—the third law of motion. Sir Isaac Newton, a seventeenth-century British scientist, came up with the **laws of motion**. The first is the law of **inertia**. Inertia is the tendency of something to continue to do whatever it's doing. Whether it's standing still or zooming through the air, Newton's law says that it's going to keep doing it unless an outside **force** acts on it. If you throw a baseball into the air, it will have the tendency to keep moving until the force of **gravity**, which brings it hurtling back to Earth, acts on it. The second law has to do with how fast things go and their direction of travel.

It's the third law of motion that helped Korso. It states that for every action, there is an equal and opposite reaction. A blast of gas shooting downward from the tail of a **rocket** pushes against the ground and causes the craft to shoot upward into the air. In the same way, the blast from Korso's weapon rocketed him into the kitchen and momentarily out of the Drej line of fire.

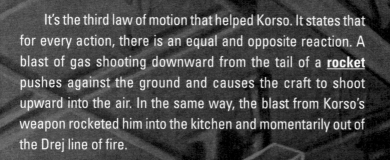

Sir Isaac Newton was one of the world's greatest scientists. His work helped to pave the way for the development of space travel. Newton discovered the law of gravity and invented the reflecting telescope. He also developed calculus, a form of mathematics important to astronomers.

Cale and Korso escape through an open hatch in a stolen fightercraft.

Korso used Newton's third law of motion to propel Cale and himself toward the *Valkyrie*. "Every action creates an equal and opposite reaction."

HUMANS IN SPACE

How are an astronaut and a deep-sea diver alike? They both have to worry about air pressure. Cale and Korso had to battle their way out of Tau-14, but the Drej weren't going to make it easy. Pursued through a ceiling vent and fired at in the landing bay, the humans barely made it out alive in a stolen fightercraft. Once outside the station, they let out a deep breath. That was when the viewing shield started to crack and they knew they were seconds away from taking their last breath.

As Cale and Korso crashed out of the craft and leaped into space unprotected, they faced some of the same difficulties as a deep-sea diver on Earth. One example is the bends, also known as decompression sickness. It's caused by a quick decrease in surrounding air pressure. Under such conditions, **nitrogen** gas oozes out of the blood and creates bubbles in the bloodstream that cut off the **oxygen** supply. It causes tremendous pain in the lungs and joints and makes the victim confused as well. Without treatment, it is usually deadly.

Korso made a good choice when he told Cale to exhale before they left the escape craft. By breathing out, they lowered the air pressure in their lungs. Holding the breath could cause another problem associated with diving, in which the air trapped in the lungs expands. The lung tears, or a bubble of air blocks a blood vessel. If the blocked vessel happens to lead to the lungs, heart, or brain—it's deadly. The duo faced other problems as well, including a major dose of **radiation** and a lack of breathable oxygen. Whether they were in deep shadows or in direct sunlight made

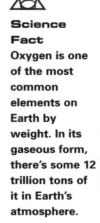

Science Fact
Oxygen is one of the most common elements on Earth by weight. In its gaseous form, there's some 12 trillion tons of it in Earth's atmosphere.

a difference, too, since they could have either been fried or frozen. Fortunately, through Korso's quick thinking and a replay of Newton's third law, they made it to the safety of the waiting *Valkyrie* in a split second. Once aboard, Korso said that Cale's blood froze. In our time, that would be a death sentence. A thousand years from now, regenerating a few quarts of blood may be routine.

Operating rooms on Earth must be as free of harmful, infection-causing bacteria as possible. The medic bay on the *Valkyrie* probably has a system for eliminating alien bacteria as well.

MEDIC BAY

Think about what it was like to get sick at the turn of the twentieth century. Many of our routine vaccines and prescription drugs had not yet been developed. There were no antibiotics and no anesthetics to be used during surgery. There were few lab tests and no **X-rays**, CAT scans, electrocardiograms, or patient computer records. To someone from the year 1900, a modern hospital would be filled with unbelievable wonders.

Now imagine what it might be like to step into a medical facility of the future. After Cale survives this harrowing spaceflight into the *Valkyrie*, what resources does Akima have at her fingertips as she cares for him? Science

Science Speak
Virtual reality is a realistic simulation of an environment by a computer.

Cybersurgery (surgery using computers and robotics) is within our technology already. It brings medical experts to patients thousands of miles away. A doctor in New York can assist during a surgery in London by computer link. That soon may be improved greatly when doctors and patients come together through virtual reality. Tiny probes inserted in a patient's body will allow the surgeon to "feel" inside without making an opening large enough to fit a hand. Computers also may do routine medical exams. The patient would wear a device that would transmit his or her information to a computer. Doctors would wear special gloves that would allow them to "touch" patients.

fiction fans are already familiar with some of the things in a space-age doctor's medical kit. The surprise is that reality is catching up to fantasy once again. Like the probe Akima uses to examine Cale, astronauts will soon carry a small wireless, hand-held instrument pack that can perform tests that include the monitoring of heart and brain function.

Computers have greatly improved medical record keeping. Soon we may go one step further by carrying our own medical information in a wallet. Cale probably carries a special card encoded with his personal genetic information. By inserting the card into a medical computer, Akima can obtain treatments and even medicines to suit Cale's individual needs.

Science Fact
For most of the time that humans have walked the Earth, the average lifespan was less than 30 years. It was about 45 years at the end of the 19th century. That number has been extended greatly, but some scientists believe the actual limit to a human lifespan is around 125 years.

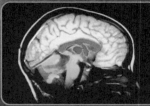

Special cells called stem cells may eventually be used to grow replacements for damaged tissue in any part of the body—even the brain.

When Cale and Korso first met, Cale was only five years old and Korso was already a soldier—yet he still seems as vital and strong as a young man. Even aging may soon be slowed by medical science. Muscle-building vaccines are in the works that can help rebuild strength in older patients and aid others with crippling diseases. It is certain that new discoveries will lead to longer lifespans and people will stay youthful longer.

Preed, Korso's sly alien first mate, lost an ear in a shoot-out with slave traders. That may be a problem for his species,

A double helix configuration is the basis of the **DNA** model. The entire genetic code for a single life form is called its genome.

but for humans, within decades, brain implants will improve the lives of people who have lost the use of arms and legs. Replacement parts will be wired directly into the patient's brain, allowing him or her to move the parts just by thinking about it. By stimulating the brain, it is likely that such parts will be able to experience a wide range of feelings. And what about staying healthy? Your teacher is right—your diet will help. Certain foods will be genetically engineered to protect people against diseases. A type of potato already exists that may do the job against a deadly disease called cholera. ◎

A gene is a little section of **DNA** that contains the information cells need to develop and do their jobs. Researchers are working to discover what each gene controls.

Cale's dad passed on a very special ring to his son. Cale also inherited something else from his father— his genes. Cale's ring was able to detect the genetic match between the young man and his father.

<CHAPTER 8>

SESHARRIM

Korso isn't searching blindly for the *Titan*. Cale has a map. It appeared on the palm of his hand after Korso tapped a special code into Sam Tucker's ring, and Cale put it back on his finger. According to the map, the first clue in the quest for the *Titan* lies on a mysterious **planet** called Sesharrim—home to an ancient race called the Gaoul. Accompanying the rest of the *Valkyrie*'s crew on the mission are Gune, the alien navigator rumored to be "self-created," and Stith, the street-wise master gunner.

A hoversled is the perfect way to get around on the water planet of Sesharrim. When we first met young Cale, he was playing with a model of one. Like most vehicles of its kind, it is at home on land or sea, and also in the air. **Hovercraft** are often used on Earth to cross small bodies of water such as the English Channel. A special wing that lifts it into the air once it reaches a certain speed supports one type of hovercraft. Others ride

GUNE

Species: *Unknown— but rumors persist that he is self-created.*

History: *Brilliant yet unconventional navigator. Was working in his own lab, trying to invent vehicles for single-celled creatures, when Korso made him an offer he couldn't refuse—to navigate one of the last remaining Earth-built vessels: the* Valkyrie.

Mission: *To decipher the map on Cale's hand and determine the best route to the* Titan.

on a cushion of air that has been forced down toward the ground by huge fans. Remember Newton's third law? The **force** of the air pushing downward lifts the craft upward. Propellers make the craft move forward.

 ### HYDROGEN

Space Fact The International Union of Pure and Applied Chemistry (IUPAC) assigns an official symbol to each element. The symbol for hydrogen is H. Henry Cavendish first recognized hydrogen as a unique gas in 1766.

No matter what transportation they use, Cale, Korso, Stith, and Akima must be im-

pressed by the sights of Sesharrim. Everywhere, huge trees float in the **atmosphere**, held in place by slender roots. On Earth, there are no floating trees, but there are certain seaweeds, such as giant kelp, that grow small, air-filled "bags," called bladders, that help the plant to float in water. It's likely that the trees of Sesharrim are also large **gas** bladders that float in air, but they are filled with **hydrogen** gas. Hydrogen is the lightest and most common chemical **element** in the **universe**. Under ordinary conditions, it is a colorless, odorless, tasteless gas.

After landing on Sesharrim, Korso is wise to caution Cale not to "clip" one of the hydrogen trees. The gas tends to explode into flame. At one time, hydrogen

Hovercraft are also called air-cushion vehicles. Those in use today may weigh over 100 tons and travel at speeds of up to 100 miles per hour. Smaller versions designed to carry fewer than ten people may race over the waves at 150 miles per hour. One of the benefits of this type of travel is that **hovercraft** can go faster on less fuel than other aircraft or ships. Hovercraft also can land on the shore or in the water. They do have one major drawback, though. They cannot operate in stormy weather. If the waves are more than five feet high, hovercraft must stay safely in port.

Gases such as carbon dioxide and argon are used in lasers. An atomic description of theses gases and all <u>elements</u> can be found on the periodic table of the elements, a table developed by Dimitri Mendeleev in 1869.

was chosen to fill lighter-than-air craft such as balloons and airships called dirigibles, but that led to disastrous fires. Now **helium** gas is preferred. Still, hydrogen is widely used in industry to treat fats and oils, refine petroleum, and produce ammonia. It is also important in low-temperature research.

IT'S ELEMENTARY

Hydrogen is one of ninety-two <u>elements</u> that occur naturally throughout the universe. An element is a substance that cannot be broken down into another element by chemical means. The smallest unit of an element that still has the properties of that element is called an <u>atom</u>.

IN THE ANDALI NEBULA

On Sesharrim, the group met up with a race of aliens called the Gaoul, and the chief Gaoul helped them to learn that the

Titan was hidden in the Andali Nebula. And what's a <u>nebula</u>, you ask? Well, a nebula is basically a huge cloud in <u>space</u>. The space between <u>stars</u>, or <u>interstellar space</u>, isn't empty. There are tiny particles of gas and dust floating around. Sometimes the shock wave from an exploding star pushes these

Space Fact
When you gaze at the Pleiades, you are looking at objects that are some 400 light-years away. In a way, you are also looking back in time. What you are actually seeing is how the cluster looked 400 years ago. It took that long for the light from the stars to reach Earth.

particles together into huge clouds. Nebula is Latin for cloud. New young stars form in clouds of hydrogen gas called emission nebulae. If you can find the __constellation__ of Taurus in the night sky, look at the area where its "shoulder" would be. There you'll see a __cluster__ of about seven stars called the Pleiades. It is a star cluster that started to form about fifty million years ago. If you had a very good telescope, you'd note that there are actually hundreds of stars in the cluster and they are surrounded by a hazy emission nebula that glows with reflected starlight.

Nebulae also form at the end of a star's life. A dying star puffs off layers of material. The glowing __ring__ the material forms is called a __planetary nebula__ because early astronomers mistook them for planets.

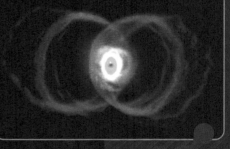

The Hourglass Nebula, MyCn18, a young planetary nebula located about 8,000 light-years away.

right: When nebulae are not lit by nearby stars, they block the stars behind them from view. These dark nebulae can sometimes be seen because their outline is illuminated from behind. **below right:** The Lagoon Nebula lies about 5,000 light-years away.

The Ring Nebula in the constellation Lyra is a good example. The faint star that produced it can still be seen at the center, but it will eventually disappear and the ring will grow wider. Planetary nebulae appear in many shapes including round, oval, ring, and dumbbell. They shine for thousands of years, then spread out and fade away.

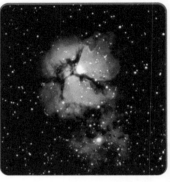

When the biggest stars explode in a **supernova**, the shock waves push space dust ahead of them to form new nebulae. In 1054, Chinese astronomers recorded a supernova in the constellation of Taurus. That explosion left behind what is now known as the Crab Nebula. It is presently at least four **light-years** across and is expanding fifty million miles each day. The Crab Nebula looks like a huge fireworks explosion in the sky. It is appropriate that it was discovered on the fourth of July. So what sort of space cloud is the Andali Nebula? It's likely that it is an emission nebula where a newborn star very much like our sun would be found—the perfect site for a new, young planet. ◎

Space Fact
Glittering in the Orion Nebula are four brilliant stars called the Trapezium, along with about 300 other young stars.

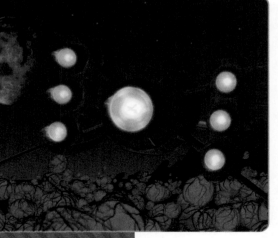

T itan A.E.'s Drej are a very unusual life form. Do you remember why? Because they are **energy** beings, giving them a number of interesting traits, starting with phosphorescent (foss-for-ESS-ent) blood. **Phosphorescence** is a form of luminescence (loom-I-NES-enss), or cool, glowing **light**, produced by certain substances after they absorb energy. For example, glow-in-the-dark stickers have to absorb light energy under a lamp before they can do their thing.

Phosphorescence was first noticed back in the 1600s, but no one paid much attention to it for the next 200 years. Then Philipp Lenard came along. He said that when a phosphorescent substance absorbs energy, some of the **electrons** in the **atoms** of the substance are sort of yanked out of their position. When the temperature is right, they return to where they belong. The energy they release in the process is seen as light without heat.

Science Fact

Phosphorescence and **fluorescence** (floor-ES-enss) are similar. The difference is that when the energy source disappears, fluorescent objects lose their glow very quickly. Something that is phosphorescent glows on and on.

DREJ STINGER

Length: *56 ft/17 m*
Wingspan: *49 ft/15 m*
Highly maneuverable alien craft equipped with defensive capability. Operated by Drej drones who are able to direct their flight through energy signals.

CENTRAL INTELLIGENCE

The Drej are organized into a worker-type society with a central intelligence—the Drej queen. In short, she does the thinking for everyone. That basic type of organization is also found on Earth. Bees typically live in colonies divided by rank. The large queen produces the eggs. There is only one queen in any hive. The job of the few hundred drones (males) is to fertilize the eggs. Many thousands of worker females build the honeycomb, collect nectar, make and store honey, clean and protect the hive, and feed and care for the queen and her offspring. The workers stay in contact with one another through scent and visual clues. For example, if a bee finds a particularly interesting field of flowers, she flies back to the hive and does a special dance. The other bees understand the meaning of the dance pattern, and they can then find the field. The Drej appear to be mentally linked and don't need to speak to each other aloud, though they may use flashes of light to communicate certain things.

Ants have a similar social organization. Some colonies may include as many as one million individuals. As with bees, there are queens, males, and workers. The workers make up the bulk of the population, but ants have an interesting twist in their system. In some colonies, a number of workers may specialize in a particular task. For example, they become soldiers. Studying the behavior of ants and bees might give the humans a little more insight into how the Drej society works.

MATTER AND ENERGY

One of the most remarkable Drej traits is that they can **convert** from beings of pure **energy** to beings made up of **matter** and back again at will. In their matter state, they aren't limited to one form either. They can become part of the ship if necessary, and when soldiers are needed, they materialize right up

Bees, like the Drej, live in colonies and are divided by rank.

Science Fact
Electromagnetic waves form when an **electric field** and a **magnetic field** pair up and travel together. Some electro-magnetic waves can travel through solids or liquids, through air, and even through space.

out of the floor. Pretty neat trick! Everything you see or feel anywhere in the universe is made up of either matter or energy. That includes you, your dog, a spaceship, the **sun**—everything. Matter is any physical thing, **solid**, liquid, or **gas**, that takes up space. Energy is the ability to do work. Let's look at the sun again. It is made up of gases that take up space. The gases are matter. The sun gives off heat and light, which are forms of energy. Energy can't be created or destroyed, only changed from one form to another.

FORCE FIELDS

Drej prison **cells** don't need locks. The prisoner is kept in place by a force field that gives a nasty shock to anyone who tries to get in or out. A field is an area over which the effects of a force are felt. For example, a gravitational field sur-rounds Earth.

The field concept was the work of British sci-entist Michael Faraday. The peculiar patterns created by the lines of force that loop in and out at the poles of a magnet inspired him. When two bodies in space exert a force on each other even though they are not in direct contact, a field is usually at work. Each type of force has a particular type of field. To cre-ate an invisible "prison door," a machine called a generator could be possibly used to produce an electrical field that would be unpleasant if not impossible to cross.

All magnets are surrounded by a magnetic field.

In a way, living things on Earth do a little matter and **energy conversion** *themselves. It starts with the sun, which converts hydrogen into helium and, in the process, gives off energy in the form of light. The light makes it to Earth, and green plants absorb and use it to manufacture their own food. We eat the plants and burn the food to produce energy, which fuels the functions of the body.*

After studying the force field that kept him imprisoned on the Drej ship, Cale found a way to defeat it.

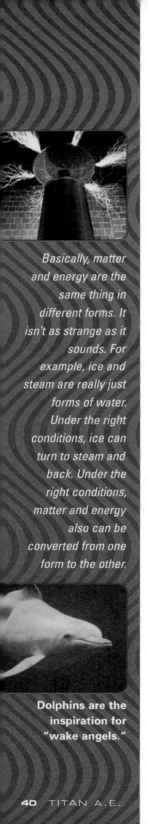

Basically, matter and energy are the same thing in different forms. It isn't as strange as it sounds. For example, ice and steam are really just forms of water. Under the right conditions, ice can turn to steam and back. Under the right conditions, matter and energy also can be converted from one form to the other.

Dolphins are the inspiration for "wake angels."

Gune used a wide variety of methods to locate objects in space and set the *Valkyrie*'s course for the Andali Nebula.

RADAR

Gune used a kind of __radar__ to search for Cale after the Drej had kidnapped him. It worked and Gune located the stolen stinger ship that Cale was piloting. But not before the navigator identified it as a stinger and Stith started to blast it. Radar was developed during World War II to detect aircraft and ships. It is a method of discovering and tracking something by bouncing __electromagnetic__

__waves__ off its surface. With radar, one can determine the position and __velocity__ of most objects.

The radar unit uses an __antenna__ to send certain electromagnetic waves in a sweeping pattern. The returning waves are picked up by a receiver and converted into a form that can be seen on a viewing screen. The distance to the object is figured out by measuring the time it took for the waves to reach the object and return. Fortunately for Cale, Gune figured out who the pilot was and the young man was rescued.

Space Speak
The term *radar* is short for radio detection and ranging.

WAKE ANGELS

When Korso allows Cale to take a test-drive of the *Valkyrie*, he describes the beautiful creatures that slipped in and out of the ship's energy wake as "wake angels." At the present time, there is no evidence that any life form could exist in the space between stars, but it is important to keep an open mind. The wake angels are patterned after a beautiful and well-loved creature of Earth's oceans—the dolphin.

Dolphins are seagoing mammals with streamlined, hairless bodies, powerful fins, high intelligence, and a built-in smile that earns them many human admirers. They are perfectly adapted to their watery world. They breathe through a single blowhole at the top of their heads, and a layer of blubber protects them from the cold.

There are some fifty species of dolphins, and many of them are known for their playfulness. They have long been noted for riding the waves created at the bows of ships. In fact, some sailors have reported that dolphins even romp in the waves created by the passage of large whales. Is it possible that there is some form of "space dolphin" surfing energy waves far out in the cosmos? It would be really nice to think so. ◎

DREJ MOTHERSHIP

Height: *25,000 ft / 7,620 m*

The heartbeat of the Drej race, the mothership houses an almost infinite source of energy and is controlled by the Drej queen, who is able to create from this energy an endless flow of Drej drones and stinger ships. The mothership's primary laser cannon has the strength to destroy planets.

CHAPTER 10

THE COLONY

NEW BANGKOK

Just when Cale was beginning to trust his new-found friends, Korso let him down—hard. He betrayed the whole human race by passing information to the Drej about where the *Titan* was hidden. The *Valkyrie* had docked with a drifter colony, New Bangkok, when Cale and Akima overheard Korso dealing with the Drej queen. As they attempted to escape from the ship, Preed fired on the pair, wounding Akima. Her only hope was help from the colonists. If humans are to travel throughout the **universe**, they'll have to learn to live with whatever resources are available. The colony of New Bangkok was put together with broken-down spacecraft. There are two main possibilities for human colonization of space. The first is to construct habitats on already existing bodies such as **planets**, moons, and **asteroids**. The second is to build habitats, like New Bangkok, from scratch out in **space**.

At the present time, a base on Earth's moon would be useful as a jumping-off place for more distant travels. The moon colony could be constructed in modules in a space station in

Akima is captured by slave traders on the slave trader ship (above), who hope to sell her to the highest bidder. After the *Valkyrie* crew rescues her, they escape and make a pit stop at New Bangkok.

Earth **orbit**. That would be easier and cheaper than launching each completed section from the planet itself. It also would be practical to use resources found on the moon. There may be pockets of ice in the deeper craters. **Minerals** could be mined and **oxygen** drawn from moon rocks. Sinking the colony under a six-foot layer of **lunar** soil would be practical for a number of reasons, including protection from extreme temperatures and **radiation**.

A system of airlocks at the surface would lead to living space, laboratories, and storage facilities. Of course, recycling would be a major part of a lunar settlement, since regular trash pickup is out of the question. There are other planets and **moons** in the solar system that could be altered to be more Earth-like through a process called **terraforming**.

The settling of moons and planets was not the only option open to space-bound humans after their planet was destroyed. Settlements in orbit offer plenty of advantages. Depending on its size, such a space colony could have a very Earth-like environment. Twenty-four-hour exposure to sunlight is a cheap and renewable source of **energy**. It would be

Space Fact
The thrust of the *Deep Space 1* ion drive is barely equal to the pressure of a sheet of paper resting on your open hand.

*Microgravity would have a few benefits in a **space orbiter**. Although most of the colony would be held at one G, certain areas could be set aside for experimental work or heavy construction. It would be a lot easier to move heavy materials in low gravity. The station itself also could be much larger than a similar structure, since weight wouldn't be a problem.*

the job of solar panels to capture sunlight and **convert** it into electric current for life support and daily needs. Huge solar mirrors could even concentrate enough solar energy to power small factories. Mirrors and panels could direct or block out light, imitating the changing of day to night. The interior of the settlement could even be landscaped with soil, flowing water, and fields of growing plants.

THE PHOENIX

Cale and Akima knew that to make it to where the *Titan* was hidden, the Ice Rings of Tigrin, they would need a spacecraft. Of all of the ships in New Bangkok, only the *Phoenix* had a chance of flying, but it was one step away from the junk heap when Cale and Akima received her from the mayor of New Bangkok. Even so, Cale was confident that with help from the colonists, he could make her fly again, particularly because her ionic vacuum drive was still intact.

Amazingly, an ion drive combines technology from television picture tubes and photo flash units. It propels a craft by

ejecting high-speed ions to deliver a very slight push, or thrust. Still, for a given amount of fuel, it can increase the craft's **velocity** ten times more than liquid or solid rocket fuels can. It isn't enough thrust to launch the craft from Earth, but it will keep it going through space for a very long distance.

Is **ion propulsion** merely a dream? Not anymore, thanks to NASA's Solar Electric Propulsion Technology Application Readiness program team (NSTAR).

PHOENIX

Length: *117 ft/36 m*
Wingspan: *110 ft/34 m*
Originally built to enable accelerated space exploration, it has long since fallen into disrepair and has become home to the Elder of drifter colony New Bangkok.

The **ion propulsion** engine is a technology that involves ionizing a gas to propel a craft.

Give It a Good Whack

The problem with the ion propulsion drive of Deep Space 1 *may have been as small as a fleck of grit. Scientists think the bit may have gotten lodged in high-voltage grids within the ion engine. As the parts of the spacecraft expanded and contracted in the extreme temperatures of space, the grit worked its way out.*

Their ionic propulsion system is presently propelling the tiny probe, *Deep Space 1* on its voyage of discovery through the solar system.

There were a few tense hours when the system was first activated. The engine shut itself off after about five minutes and it remained off despite the engineers' attempts to start it. The next opportunity to correct the problem presented itself two weeks later. *Deep Space 1*'s engine started up immediately and has been going without a hitch since then. ◎

Deep Space 1 (DS1), the first of NASA's New Millennium Program missions, is testing 12 advanced technologies and instruments on a journey through the solar system.

CHAPTER 11

TITAN FOUND

a fter a shaky start, Cale and Akima set a course for the Andali Nebula, unaware that the *Valkyrie* is already out there— searching. Aboard the *Valkyrie*, Gune and Stith are confused by Cale and Akima's disappearance. Their confusion mounts as the *Phoenix* shows up and Korso orders Gune to sneak after it into the dangerous Ice Rings of Tigrin.

Ring structures are not uncommon in the universe. Several **planets** in our own solar system have **rings**, but the most out-standing are the bright ice rings of Saturn, and they are a good example of how ring systems work. The ring particles seem to be made up of billions of bits of ice, each in its own **orbit** around the **gas** giant. They range in size from specks to boulders, with a few elephant-sized chunks likely. Saturn's rings are remarkably thin. Even though they're more than 150,000 miles in diameter, they're no more than a mile deep. What would happen if you swept all of the icy bits and pieces into a single body? It would be less than sixty-five

Science Fact
Saturn's rings are made up of many small pieces of ice, each in a specific orbit around the planet.

STITH

Species: *Mantrin*
History: *Cranky master gunner. Trained on the mean streets of Solbrecht, where her keen eye and lust for extreme firepower earned her a vicious reputation.*
Mission: *To protect and serve, but only when she's in the mood.*

miles across. No one knows for certain why the rings formed and how long they have been in place. It's likely that they have changed a great deal from the time that they developed, and that Saturn's beautiful ring system will look quite different in the future.

If Sam Tucker's plan was to hide the *Titan* in a region that might support a populated planet, a field of ice **crystals** was a great idea. For human life to survive, water is a must. Water is a clear, tasteless, odorless liquid. In its **solid** and liquid forms, it covers about seventy percent of Earth's surface. Water vapor is in the **atmosphere**. Even human beings are water-filled. The life-giving fluid makes up over ninety percent of blood plasma, eighty percent of muscle tissue, and more than half of most other tissues. Unlike other substances, when water is frozen, it expands. That is because of the way the molecules line up under low temperatures. Ice crystals are made up of open, hexagonal (six-sided) columns. Because these crystals are honeycombed with open areas, ice is not as packed with **matter**, or as **dense**, as an equal amount of water.

Crystals have different physical properties, including hardness and their ability to carry heat and electricity. These properties make some crystals handy for grinding and polishing very hard materials and also for use in space communications. For example, quartz has electrical properties that make it perfect for use in radios and other devices.

Crystals form by **evaporation** or **freezing**—a process called **crystallization**. A crystal is a solid body with natural flat outer surfaces. The shape of the outer surfaces is determined by the inner structure of the crystal. The atoms that make up the inner structure are organized in a pattern called the crystalline lattice.

We see objects because of the light reflected from their surfaces. The color of a material depends on whether it reflects light of a certain wavelength or absorbs it. For example, most plants absorb all the colors in sunlight except green, which is reflected away. So that is what we see and why most plants appear green to us.

REFLECTION AND REFRACTION

Have you ever visited the hall of mirrors at a carnival? It can be very easy to get lost within. When Akima is expertly piloting the *Phoenix* through the ice rings, she realizes that Korso is close behind. As she moves between the spiraling ice crystals, the ship is reflected in one crystal surface after another. Akima quickly decides to use the many reflections to confuse Korso and get him to follow an image of the *Phoenix* instead of the real one. Her plan begins with a little knowledge of the **electromagnetic spectrum**. Reflection is the return of an electromagnetic wave from a surface that doesn't absorb it. Light waves in the visible range generally travel in straight lines. A ray of **light** that strikes a reflective surface straight on returns straight back to where it originated. If a ray strikes a reflective surface at an angle, it is reflected in an opposite direction. Smooth, polished surfaces, such as that of a mirror and in some cases ice, are highly reflective.

Rattlesnakes, also known as pit vipers, have tiny sensory pits that can detect infrared energy from warm-blooded prey much the same as the infrared sensors on the *Valkyrie* track their human prey on the *Phoenix*.

Refraction results from the fact that light travels at different speeds through different substances. For example, let's say a ray of light hits a glass of water at an angle. One part of the ray hits the water before the rest and slows down. In this way, the light is bent as it enters the glass.

You can observe this for yourself by dropping a pencil in a half-filled glass of water and checking it out from the side. The pencil looks as though it is bent. Of course it isn't the pencil, but the light rays that have changed. Refraction is used in some telescopes. **Reflection** and **refraction** also help the *Phoenix* to appear to be where it is not. Due to refraction, the ship seems to be going in one direction when it is actually moving in another. Gune is bewildered when, for a moment, the ship they are following appears to be behind them.

It is possible for light rays to be bounced around within an object. For example, a ray that is passing from one substance into another substance that is less dense may be bounced back at the boundary between the two. This is called total internal reflection, and it is what makes a diamond glitter so brightly. Something similar happens in raindrops when rays of sunlight enter them. The sunlight breaks up into its many colors and, with luck, you may see a rainbow.

The principles of reflection and refraction are used in satellite dish technology.

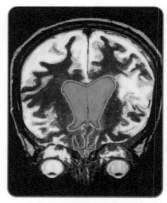

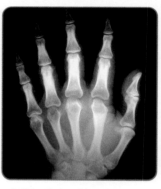

SEEING RED

For a while, Akima's plan worked perfectly, but Korso isn't easily fooled. He knows his eyes may be playing tricks on him in the ice rings, making him unable to tell the difference between the real *Phoenix* and its reflection. But he has another trick up his sleeve. The **infrared** scanner on the *Valkyrie* can easily pick up the heat signature from the *Phoenix,* and he orders Gune to use it.

Our eyes are designed to detect visible light, but there are many other forms of **electromagnetic radiation** that we can't see. These include **gamma rays**, **X-rays**, **ultraviolet** rays, **infrared** rays, **microwaves**, and **radio waves**. The difference between these types of radiation is their wavelength or **frequency**—the number of waves that are squeezed into a given space. The wavelength is shorter and the frequency greater at the high-energy, gamma ray end of the spectrum.

Science Fact

Radio waves, television waves, and microwaves are all part of the electromagnetic spectrum.

Infrared radiation has longer wavelengths and lower frequencies than visible light. We can't see it, but we sometimes feel it as heat. Warm up in sunlight or near a fire and you are in the path of infrared energy. Anything that has a measurable temperature above absolute zero radiates in the infrared. That includes everything from ice cubes to the family dog. But wait—if ice gives off infrared radiation, how could Gune track the *Phoenix* in a whole field of ice? The warmer the

object, the more infrared radiation it gives off. With its interior heat, the *Phoenix* would stand out like a sore thumb.

Korso is determined to catch up to the *Phoenix*, and Akima is determined to lose him. As Cale screams for her to pull up, she slips the ship between two huge ice crystals and down a long ice tunnel, then pulls out into open space. It's then that Cale gets a glimpse of something hidden among the glittering ice. Akima turns the *Phoenix,* and a huge bronze orb comes into view. At last—the *Titan* has been found!

HOLOGRAMS

Slowly, carefully, Akima docks the *Phoenix* with the *Titan*. With Cale in the lead, they slip through the **airlock** and into the giant craft. It is a mammoth globe that extends as far as the eye can see. The air inside is crisp and chilly. Lining the curved walls are hundreds of thousands of glass vials. Each is labeled with a name—bottle-nosed dolphin... leopard... elephant... butterfly.

Cale's father appeared before him as a holographic image.

Stepping onto a central platform, Cale finds the toy **hovercraft** he played with so long ago when the Earth still existed. He touches the control panel and suddenly he is standing face to face with his father, Sam Tucker. Sadly he realizes that the image before him is not real. It is a **hologram**.

⊕

Science Speak
The term *hologram* is from the Greek words "holos" for whole and "gramma" for message.

Holograms are three-dimensional images produced by a **laser** light source. The hologram of Sam Tucker that appeared to his son was an example of a reflection hologram. Cale was able to walk around it and see an image from every angle. It is produced when a continuous-wave gas laser light bounces a beam off a mirror and through a splitter, creating two beams. Each beam then passes through beam spreaders. One beam spreads over the back of a gas-sensitive plate, while the other beam lights the plate from the front. Together the two create an image.

Holograms are widely used for medical imaging, for security (they can't be copied), to store information, and even as an art form. Unfortunately, the hologram of Sam Tucker couldn't warn Cale that Korso had finally found them. With a blast from his laser, the captain destroyed the hologram generator.

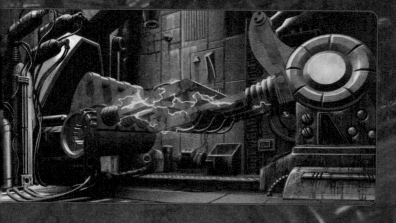

To re-route the system, Cale must lock several circuit breakers in place. When the electric current in a circuit, a closed path that carries electric current, becomes too great, the circuit breaker stops it.

THE DREJ RETURN

"You can't beat the Drej. No one can. They're pure energy." Ominous words from Korso—but why are energy beings so powerful? As we've discussed, energy is the ability or capacity to do work or to produce change. But did you know that it takes many forms, including light, heat, sound, electricity, chemical energy, and, apparently, scary-looking blue aliens like the Drej?

The study of **physics** is loaded with laws governing energy. One is the law of **conservation**. It states that energy can be **convert**ed from one form to another, but it can't be created or destroyed. In a fire, the chemical energy in the fuel is not completely burned away, but changed to heat and light. Energy also can be converted into matter, which, in turn, can be converted into energy. What this means is that the law of conservation applies to the Drej, making them a very dangerous enemy since they cannot be destroyed— only converted into something else. But Cale has an idea. The *Titan* has been drained of the energy needed to start its **reactor**. If Cale is correct, he can reroute the system to use Drej energy, draining the aliens and powering the *Titan*. ©

top: An AC/DC electrical conversion substation.
above: Drej stingers swarm around the spaceship *Titan*.

A high current triggers a special device in the breaker that separates a pair of contacts, interrupting the current flow. The circuit breaker can be reset immediately afterward. Unfortunately, when circuit breaker #3 malfunctions, Cale has no choice but to go outside of the *Titan* to repair it. Under heavy Drej fire, he seems to be doomed, when Korso shows up again—this time to give his life to save humanity.

TITAN THE ARK

Through Korso's sacrifice and with the help of Stith and Gune, Cale and Akima are able to set up *Titan*'s control unit. As the Drej fire on the huge ship, their **energy** streams into its **reactor**, which begins to spin and glow. The energy stream changes from blue to brilliant red. By the time the aliens realize that their energy is being converted and absorbed, it is toolate.They are destroyed, and the stage is set for a new Earth tobe created.

When Cale and Akima first boarded the *Titan*, they saw hundreds and thousands of vials each labeled with the name of a different animal. In a sense, the ship is a huge ark. Its stored vials contain the precious **DNA** of Earth's living things that will be used to **clone** plants and animals to populate the new Earth. Cloning is the production of a newborn creature from any **cell** of a preexisting creature. Actually, cloning has been around for a long time. It is a natural method of reproduction for certain life forms, such as some bacteria and yeast. Even some more complex life forms make exact copies

Science Fact
The oldest **fossils** of living things on Earth are not quite four billion years old. The ancestors of today's reptiles first appeared at least 300 million years ago.

Science Fact
In 1970, Dr. John Gurdon transplanted the cell of a tadpole into a frog egg, which resulted in the birth of a perfectly normal frog.

of themselves, like some snails and shrimp. Aphids are insects that produce several generations of clones before slipping in a group born of male/female interaction.

It requires two **cells** to perform a **nuclear transfer**. The nucleus is removed from an unfertilized egg to get rid of as much genetic information as possible. The donor cell is put into a dormant, or sleeping state, then transplanted inside the egg. Once the egg cell begins forming an embryo, it is placed into a substitute (surrogate) mother. In general, clones are genetically identical to the parents, but new research shows there is some room for change.

Cloning is in its early development, but the process might help to preserve endangered species. It could be an option for animals that do not breed successfully in captivity. At the present time, however, a living, breathing substitute mother is still necessary to develop and give birth to the baby.

Even if two beings start out the same, the conditions under which each is born and raised make a big difference in the result. It's possible that Einstein's clone could fail fifth-grade math!

Science Fact
Dr. Hans Spemann first discussed cloning in the laboratory in 1938. He suggested removing the nucleus from an unfertilized egg and replacing it with the nucleus of a viable egg. Called nuclear transfer, the process works.

In 1996, Dr. Ian Wilmut and his team cloned Dolly, the first sheep developed from the adult cells of another, six-year-old sheep. Born in July 1996, she appears to be normal and has given birth to several lambs of her own in the standard manner. Mother and offspring are all doing fine. There is some concern, though, that Dolly's lifespan may be shorter than that of a sheep born under natural conditions. After all, when she was born, her cellular clock was set to age six.

A NEW HOME

Recent research has shown that planetary systems are not uncommon in the Milky Way. Using a technology far beyond our current capabilities, the *Titan* began a process that has been repeated naturally over and over since the **universe** began. Swirling **gases** and ice **crystals** spin into a huge sphere. Taking

Using unbelievable amounts of energy, the *Titan* sped up the process. The *Titan* also must have produced an oxygen-rich atmosphere for the young planet. Without **oxygen**, there would be no life as we know it on Earth, and without life, there would be no free oxygen.

the *Titan* to a safe distance, Cale and Akima watch as their new **planet** roils in a molten mass, then cools. Clouds gather in its newly formed **atmosphere**. Finally, the *Titan* lands on a primitive landscape and Cale and Akima view their world from a cliff over a newborn ocean.

The formation of a solar system like ours starts with a cloud of **interstellar** gas and dust called the solar **nebula**. Something, perhaps a nearby **supernova**, sends a shock wave through the cloud, setting it in motion. As it whirls, the cloud forms a **dense**, hot center. Within 100,000 years, a **protostar** takes shape, gathering in most but not all of the rotating cloud. What is left forms a flattened disk around the

star. As the central **mass** continues to heat up, the disk cools. Dust particles in the planet-forming nebula crash together to form larger particles, growing to the size of boulders in **orbit** around the young star. As their size increases, so does their **gravity**. The very biggest chunks start sweeping up tinier particles in their path.

There was little if any oxygen in the atmosphere of the early Earth. No **ozone** layer shielded living things from harmful solar **radiation**. Without the *Titan*, planet Earth had to form a life-supporting atmosphere the old-fashioned way.

About one million years after the first stirrings in the protostar, nuclear **fusion** begins and the **sun** roars to life, producing a very strong solar wind that forces leftover gases outward. The gravity of the smaller infant planets, or planetesimals, isn't enough to hold the gas, and they end up as rocky planets. Larger planetesimals hold on to the gas and become gas giants. After millions of years of bombardment by leftover rocky bits and pieces, the planets reach their final size and the solar system becomes stable.

Eventually tiny living things, **microorganisms**, developed in the sea. These marine creatures took in **carbon dioxide** and released plenty of oxygen. Over many millions of years, **ozone**, a form of oxygen, built up in a protective layer around the planet and the atmosphere became suitable for oxygen-breathing life. Now the atmosphere is made up of mostly **nitrogen** and oxygen, with traces of argon gas, carbon dioxide, and water.

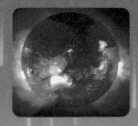

left: **The formation of a new planetary system begins with the birth of the central star, or "sun."** *right top:* **An earthlike planet begins to form when bits of matter draw together and continue to sweep up the matter in its path. Incredible pressure causes the interior of the new planet to heat up, and molten lava spews across its surface. The lava then cools to form a hard surface crust.** *right middle:* **As lava rises to the surface, it brings gases as well. The gases begin to form the early atmosphere.** *right bottom:* **Water vapor in the atmosphere cools and falls as rain, eventually forming oceans. The first living things appear in the oceans.**

the planet and the atmosphere became suitable for oxygen-breathing life. Now the atmosphere is made up of mostly **nitrogen** and oxygen, with traces of argon gas, carbon dioxide, and water.

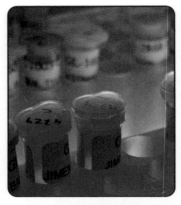

PLANET EARTH

Standing close together, Akima and Cale stare out at the newly formed planet. In a soft voice, Akima asks Cale what he will call it. After a moment he responds.

"I think I'll call it… Bob."

Perhaps Cale will change his mind, but as the two stand side by side on the cliff, scores of human craft are making their way toward their new home. Still, humanity will never forget its planet of origin. As you and I both know, Earth is a very special place. It is the largest of the inner rocky planets, and the only one in the solar system known to support life. It whirls on its own axis at nearly 1,000 miles per hour, making one complete turn in about twenty-four hours. The planet also speeds around the **sun** at almost twenty miles per second, taking 365 days to complete the trip. Because it is tilted on its axis, during its

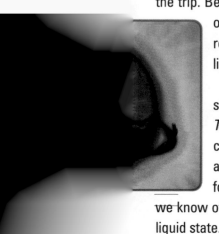

orbit, different areas on the planet receive different amounts of direct sunlight. This is why we have seasons.

Planet Bob is probably similar in structure to Earth. It's likely that the *Titan*'s designers would have planned to create a world that would be comfortable and familiar for Earth-based life forms. Presently, Earth is the only planet we know of that has great amounts of water in a liquid state. It also has a great deal of fresh water frozen into large icecaps at both poles. We live on

Science Fact
Since scientists can't actually see inside the planet, they learn about it by studying sound waves caused by earthquakes.

Earth's hard outer crust, which is made up of rocky materials such as quartz and feldspar. The crust is like a big jigsaw puzzle of huge plates that move very slowly, producing activity such as volcanic eruptions and earthquakes. Over millions of years, this movement combined with erosion has changed the surface features of the planet.

Space Speak
The solar wind is a stream of ionized hydrogen gas and helium gas that races outward from the sun at between 200 and 400 miles per second.

In *Titan A.E.*, humans lost their home planet and all they held dear. Due to Sam Tucker's vision, they gained a second chance. Using DNA stored in the *Titan*, humans populated the new planet with life forms such as mammals, insects, and reptiles. Once again, fish swam in the seas and birds flew in the air. But of course the story is science fiction—it couldn't really happen. Or could it? Many of the concepts presented in the film are based on real science with a big dash of imagination. At the present time, we can only guess what the future will hold in store for our small planet spinning around an average star near the edge of our **galaxy**. One thing is certain, Earth's sun won't last forever. Whether the threat comes from the Drej or from solar death throes, if life from this planet is to survive, like Cale and Akima, we will someday need to find a new home... out there among the stars. ◎

Bob doesn't appear to have a moon, so the oceans on humanity's new home may not experience tides. The moon's gravity is the main cause of the tides in Earth's oceans. Our satellite is also slowing Earth's **rotation** by nearly two milliseconds each century. About 900 million years ago, days were only eighteen hours long and there were some 480 of them in a year.

TITAN GLOSSARY

aerobraking
A fuel-saving method of slowing down a spacecraft. The craft flies through a planet's upper atmosphere. The interaction between the atmosphere and a wide, saucer-shaped aerobrake at the nose of the ship slows the craft down.

airlock
A compartment used when moving between areas of different air pressure. To leave an orbiting spacecraft, an astronaut enters an airlock through an inner door, or hatch, which is sealed behind him or her to protect the air-filled ship. An outer door is then opened, and the astronaut is free to leave the craft for airless space.

antenna
The part of an instrument that sends and/or receives energy signals.

artificial gravity
The feeling of having weight within a spacecraft that is created by the craft's rotation or other forms of movement.

asteroid
Small planetlike rocky objects. The largest, Ceres, is about 600 miles across, but most asteroids are a mile or two across.

asteroid belt
A 150-million-mile-wide ring made up of thousands of asteroids that circle the sun between the orbits of Mars and Jupiter. Many asteroids exist outside of the asteroid belt.

astrobiology
Study of life other than that on Earth. To date, no alien life forms have been found. Also called exobiology.

astronomical unit
A measurement that is the average distance from the sun to the Earth, or about 93 million miles. Also called AUs, they are used to measure distances between objects within the solar system.

atmosphere
A layer of gas or gases that surround a star or planet. Earth's atmosphere is made up mainly of nitrogen (N) and oxygen (O).

atom
The smallest unit of an element that still has the properties of that element.

big bang
A theory of how the universe as we know it began. According to the theory, the big bang was the exact moment, between 10 and 20 billion years ago, that our universe came into existence. It exploded outward from a tiny pinpoint and expanded to the universe we know now. George Lemaitre first proposed this theory in 1927.

carbon dioxide
A colorless, odorless gas also written as CO_2.

cell
1. The smallest unit of an organism that can function independently. Most animal cells are made up of a central unit called a nucleus, surrounded by a fluid called cytoplasm that contains various tiny structures. The cells are surrounded by a skin-like outer covering called a membrane. Plant cells are constructed differently from animal cells.
2. A small room such as one in a prison.

centripetal force
The force that is directed toward the center of an area and that acts on an object such as a planet, satellite, comet, or spacecraft, keeping it moving in a curved path around a central point.

clone
A newborn creature developed from any cell of a single creature that is already alive.

cluster
A group. A star cluster is an area in space where there are a large number of associated stars compared to the surrounding space. There are two main types of star clusters: globular clusters and open clusters.

combustion area
An area where the process of burning takes place.

comet
A small, icy body of dust and gas probably left over from the formation of the solar system. A comet orbits the sun. When it first nears the heat of the sun, a comet develops a glowing halo of gas. As it draws closer to the sun, it may develop two long tails, a curved dust tail, and a long gas tail streaming out from behind.

conservation
The preservation or maintenance of an object, a substance, or energy. Also, the attempt to keep something as unchanged as possible.

constellation
Any of the star patterns in the sky that have been named after people, animals, or objects. There are eighty-eight different constellations. In modern astronomy, a constellation is generally considered the entire area of the sky where the star pattern is found.

convert
To change anything into a different form.

core
The center of a planet, moon, or star. Earth is thought to have a small, solid inner core made up mostly of iron and nickel surrounded by a liquid outer core.

crystal
A solid body with naturally flat outer surfaces. The shape of the outer surfaces depends on the inner structure. The inner structure is formed by a pattern of tiny units such as atoms.

crystallization
Process of forming crystals.

density
A measure of how much matter is contained in a given space. If two objects are the same size but one is more dense, the denser object will be heavier.

DNA
A material that helps cells in living things know exactly what they are supposed to do. A gene is a little section of DNA, and it contains the information that cells need to develop and to do their jobs. For example, one gene may tell the eyes to be blue, while another tells the hair to be curly. DNA stands for **D**(eoxyribo)**N**(ucleic)**A**(cid).

docking
The joining of two or more spacecraft in space.

electric field
An area of space where a force has been generated by electric charge. Charge is a property or characteristic of matter. It takes two forms—positive and negative.

electromagnetic energy
Waves of electrical and magnetic energy that travel at right angles to each other at the speed of light. These include X-rays, ultraviolet light, visible light, infrared radiation, and radio waves.

electromagnetic radiation
(see electromagnetic energy)

electromagnetic spectrum
The different types of energy that travel in waves, arranged in order of wavelength. The longest waves are radio waves, while the shortest are gamma rays.

electromagnetic waves
(see electromagnetic energy)

electron
A part of an atom. An atom is made up of three types of particles: protons, neutrons, and electrons. Protons and neutrons form the center, or nucleus, of an atom. Electrons whirl in orbit around the nucleus.

element
Any one of more than 100 substances that are each made up entirely of atoms of the same type, and that cannot be broken down into simpler substances. Gold (Au), iron (Fe), and neon (Ne) are all elements. The four most common elements on Earth are oxygen (O), silicon (Si), aluminum (Al), and iron (Fe).

energy
The ability to do work.

energy conversion
The change of one form of energy to another form of energy and/or matter.

entry interface
The point at which a spacecraft reenters the atmosphere of a planet.

equator
An imaginary line midway between the poles of a body such as a planet or a star. The equator divides the body into two equal halves known as the northern and southern hemispheres.

evaporation
Changing from a liquid into a gas, usually as a result of heating.

Fahrenheit
A temperature scale measured in degrees. On this scale at sea level, water freezes at 32 degrees and boils at 212 degrees. The Fahrenheit scale is generally not used in astronomy. The temperature scales commonly used in astronomy and other sciences are the centigrade and Kelvin scales.

fluorescence
A form of cool glowing light, produced by certain substances after they absorb energy. When the energy source disappears, fluorescent objects lose their glow very quickly.

fossil
The remains or traces of an organism that lived long ago, such as a bone or hardened footprint of a dinosaur. Fossils are generally preserved in the Earth's crust.

force
An outside influence that can act on matter so that it moves, changes direction, or changes shape. Four forces are known in the universe: gravity, electromagnetism, and the strong and weak forces. The last two are only noticeable over very tiny distances within individual atoms.

freezing
Changing from liquid to solid state due to the loss of heat.

frequency
The number of times something occurs within a given space in a given amount of time.

FTL
*An abbreviation for **F**aster **T**han **L**ight.*

fusion
The joining together of two or more substances to form a new substance. Nuclear fusion takes place in the center of stars under very high temperature and pressure. Tremendous amounts of energy are released in the process. Fusion is the energy source in stars.

G
A unit of force due to speeding up— also known as acceleration. At the surface of the Earth, the acceleration due to gravity is one "G."

galaxy
A huge spinning system made up of gas, dust, and billions of stars, plus all of the planets, satellites, comets, and asteroids associated with those stars, all held together by gravity. Our solar system is part of the Milky Way galaxy.

gamma ray
The form of electromagnetic radiation with the highest frequency and the shortest wavelength. This radiation can be extremely dangerous to living things. Fortunately, Earth's atmosphere absorbs most gamma rays from space.

gas
A form of matter. Gas has no definite shape, but will take the shape of the container in which it is held and fill the entire container. It will scatter if not contained. Much of the matter in the universe is hydrogen (H) gas.

gravity
The force of attraction between every object and every other object. The more massive an object is, the more the effect of its gravity may be felt. The greater the distance between objects, the less the effect of gravity may be felt. The force of gravity is measured as weight.

helium
A colorless, odorless element that usually exists as a gas. The symbol for helium is He.

hologram
A three-dimensional image produced by a laser light source.

hovercraft
A vehicle made for traveling over land or water on a cushion of air.

hydrogen
The lightest and most common element in the universe.

hydroponics
A method of growing plants without soil. The plants are raised in water or a special material containing nutrients.

inertia
The tendency of something to continue doing what it is doing and to resist changing, whether it is moving or at rest.

infrared
Part of the electromagnetic spectrum that has a wavelength a little longer than that of visible red light. Although we generally can't see it without special instruments, we can usually feel it as heat.

interstellar space
The space between stars. Although interstellar space is mostly empty, it does contain clouds of gas and dust.

ion propulsion
A form of deep space propulsion that moves the craft by ejecting high-speed ions to deliver a very slight thrust, or push. Ions are atoms that have gained or lost an electron or proton and so have a positive or negative electric charge.

laser
A term for light amplification by stimulated emission of radiation. That means that a laser device produces a very narrow, high-energy beam of light. The light is produced (or stimulated) by an active medium such as ruby.

laws of motion
Three laws of physics developed by Sir Isaac Newton to explain relationships between force and motion.

light
Electromagnetic radiation that travels in waves at a speed of 186,000 miles per second. Visible light is the part of the electromagnetic spectrum that is visible to the human eye. Its color is determined by its wavelength.

light-year
A measure of distance. A light-year is the distance light travels in empty space during one Earth year.

lunar
Anything that has to do with the moon is called lunar. For example, the lunar surface is the hard, outer crust of the moon.

magnetic field
An area found around a magnet or an electric current that can affect objects within the area. Such a field includes measurable magnetic force and magnetic poles.

manned maneuvering unit
A device worn by astronauts that allows them to move freely in space outside of their craft. The unit usually works by small gas-powered rockets.

mantle
The region of a planet between the core and the outer crust.

mass
The amount of matter in an object or substance.

matter
Any substance that has mass and takes up space.

M.E.T.
An abbreviation for Mission Elapsed Time or the amount of time that has passed since a particular spacecraft was launched.

metal ores
A mineral or combination of minerals from which a metal can be mined or extracted. A metal is a substance that is usually a good conductor of electricity. It can be melted or molded into forms such as thin sheets or wires. Copper (Cu) and gold (Au) are metals.

microgravity
What it is called when the force of gravity is weak. Astronauts in orbit are exposed to microgravity. It results in a feeling of weightlessness.

microorganism
A living thing so small that it can be seen only through a microscope or other special instrument.

microwave
A high-frequency electromagnetic wave between infrared and short-wave radio wavelengths on the electromagnetic spectrum.

mineral
A naturally occurring, nonliving solid substance that has a unique chemical composition and crystal structure.

mission control
A command center where scientists monitor and direct activities during a space mission.

moon
A natural satellite in orbit around a planet.

nebula
A cloud of gas and dust in space. Some nebulae glow, while others are completely dark.

neutron star
A small collapsed star made up mainly of very closely packed neutrons. Neutrons are tiny particles found in the center, or nucleus, of an atom. Neutron stars are so dense that a teaspoonful of one would weigh more than one billion tons.

nitrogen
A chemical element that usually exists as a gas. It is the most common gas in Earth's atmosphere. The symbol for nitrogen is N.

nuclear transfer
Removing the nucleus from an unfertilized egg and replacing it with the nucleus of an egg that is capable of reproducing.

orbit
The path of an object in space that is moving around another object in space.

oxygen
A chemical element that usually exists as a gas. Oxygen (O) makes up about 21% of Earth's atmosphere.

ozone
An unstable or easily changeable form of oxygen. When ozone is found near the surface of Earth, it is considered a dangerous pollutant. High in the atmosphere, however, there is a layer of ozone that absorbs dangerous ultraviolet rays from the sun and so protects living things from these rays.

phosphorescence
A cool, glowing light produced by certain substances after they have absorbed energy. When the energy source disappears, phosphorescent materials continue to glow for some time.

physics
The study of matter and energy and of the interactions between them.

planet
A body in space that orbits a star in a nearly circular orbit. There are nine large, or principal, planets in our solar system. Asteroids are often called minor planets, or planetoids.

planetary nebula
An often rounded cloud or ring of gas that is blown away from a star during the last stages of the star's life.

protostar
A star in the process of forming from a cloud of gas and dust.

pulsar
A rapidly spinning neutron star. Narrow beams of energy radiate from the poles of pulsars.

radar
A method of locating objects and determining their position, velocity, or physical characteristics using high-frequency radio waves. Radar stands for **ra**(dio) **d**(etecting) **a**(nd) **r**(anging).

radiation
The emission of energy in the form of rays (thin, narrow beams) or waves.

radio wave
A form of electromagnetic radiation. Radio waves are long, rather low-energy waves.

reactor
A contained area where a nuclear chain reaction is started and controlled. The energy resulting from the chain reaction can be used as a power source.

reentry
The return of a spacecraft into the Earth's atmosphere.

reflection
An image that has been bounced back from a surface. You can see your image, or reflection, in a mirror because the light waves leaving your face are bounced off the mirrored surface and back to your eye. The moon shines with reflected sunlight.

refraction
The bending of light as it passes through substances of different densities, such as the air and a glass lens.

refugee
A person who flees from oppression or persecution in search of safety or freedom.

ring
A swarm of small particles circling a planet. The particles can be as small as a speck of dust or as large as a house. Each follows its own orbital path about the planet.

rocket
A vehicle that travels in space and is usually propelled by a fuel that is burned to produce hot gases.

rotation
Turning around on a central point or axis. For example, the Earth rotates on its axis once about every 24 hours. The axis is an imaginary line drawn through our planet from the north to south poles.

rotational speed
The rate of speed at which a planet or other rotating space object turns. Earth's rotational speed is about 1,000 miles per hour.

satellite
An object that circles a larger object in space. The moon is a natural satellite of Earth.

scramjet
A high-speed jet that burns oxygen, which is scooped from the atmosphere as fuel. Scramjet is short for **s**upersonic **c**ombustion **ramjet**.

solid
A state in which matter has a definite shape and volume.

space
The area that begins outside of Earth's atmosphere.

space orbiter
A craft that is designed to travel to and remain in orbit for a given amount of time.

space-time
A way of describing the universe in four dimensions. It includes three dimensions of space (height, width, and depth) and the fourth dimension of time.

star
A glowing body of gases that produces energy as the result of fusion reactions at its core.

sun
An average star that is also the central body of our solar system. The sun is approximately 864,000 miles in diameter.

supernova
A tremendous explosion usually caused by the collapse of the core of a giant star.

terraforming
The transformation of a planet or moon to make it more Earth-like.

UFO
The term used to describe an object in the sky that cannot be easily explained. Some people think UFOs are alien spacecraft, but they are usually discovered to be satellites, meteors, lightning, or glowing gas. UFO is an abbreviation for **U**nidentified **F**lying **O**bject.

ultraviolet waves
Electromagnetic radiation that has a wavelength shorter than visible light and is situated just beyond violet light on the spectrum. We cannot see ultraviolet radiation.

universe
All the energy, matter, and space that exists.

velocity
A measurement of motion. To figure out velocity, you have to know how far something has gone, how long it took to cover the distance, and the direction it was traveling.

wavelength
The distance from one point in a wave to the next similar point—for example, from one low point to the next low point.

weightlessness
The absence of measurable weight. Space travelers experience weightlessness because they are falling freely without anything (such as the atmosphere or ground) to stop or slow their fall.

wormhole
In theory, a deformity in space-time that is thought to link two black holes. If wormholes actually exist (none has ever been discovered), astronomers suggest that they would probably be very unstable.

X-ray
A form of electromagnetic energy found between ultraviolet and gamma rays, with a very short wavelength and high frequency.

INDEX

RESOURCES

Check out the websites below for some cool "space time" on the net.

http://StarChild.gsfc.nasa.gov/docs/starchild/
Space info and interactive activities for kids

www.astronomical.org/framemain.htm
Plenty of astronomical info

www.starport.com
Get your questions answered first hand

www.esrin.esa.it
European Space Agency

www.nasa.gov
NASA homepage

www.jpl.nasa.gov
Jet Propulsion Laboratory homepage

www.nasm.edu
National Air & Space Museum

www.planetary.org
The Planetary Society

www.seti-inst.edu
SETI Institute

www.seds.org
Students for Exploration and Development of Space

www.deepspace.ucsb.edu
Good overview of the planets and their moons

www.spacezonew.com
For the serious space buff

www.Marsacademy.com
All the info you'll need for your upcoming trip to Mars

www.jpl.nasa.gov/basics
Basic spaceflight learner's workbook

www.inconstantmoon.com
Plenty of facts about the moon and its phases

www.tufts.edu/as/wright_center/fellows/georgepage.html
Uses "woman in the moon" to identify sites

http://astro.princeton.edu/~frei/catalog.htm
Galaxy catalog

http://comets.amsmeteors.org
Info on comets and meteors

www.ksc.nasa.gov
Kennedy Space Center